100 POEMS TO HELP YOU RELAX

100 POEMS TO HELP YOU RELAX

EDITED BY LIZ ISON

BATSFORD

Introduction

I sincerely hope that *100 Poems to Help You Relax* will create and diffuse feelings of relaxation, relief and comfort, or as John Keats put it so well, that you will find yourself transported on 'the viewless wings of poesy'.

You might have opened this book because you are feeling a bit worn down, stressed or struggling. Or maybe you are already relaxed and would like to prolong the feeling with some poetry reading. Whether a relaxed state is elusive right now or within easy reach, you have made an excellent decision to turn to poetry. Poems at their best can distil, intensify, clarify and inspire.

I would describe a state of relaxation as being a sort of equilibrium between our inner and outer worlds. We recognize it by how we feel inside: calm, centred and in control. We'll also know it by the absence of stress or the feeling that fills us after worries subside.

It is not easy to 'turn on' a state of relaxation and people pursue different strategies or activities in search of it. You might feel relaxed while enjoying a meal out with friends or discover it in a more solitary activity like reading a book or pottering in the garden. It could mean slowing down but it can also be found while running round the park. You won't be surprised to know that I find reading poetry can help me relax!

Anxiety, worry, unease, fear or a sense of foreboding: however we name it, and whether short-lived or chronic, these are feelings that are part of the human experience to a greater or lesser extent. Worry or anxiety can be useful or even protective responses to a perceived or real threat but can also hamper us. Fear might stop us from enjoying our lives to the full. It could prevent us following our desires, block the flow of love between ourselves and others, or curtail our potential. The poetry in this collection articulates what it feels like to be stuck in those emotional states but also describes ways of freeing us from these trapped places.

So can reading a poem really help people to let go of their anxieties? When someone is going through difficult times it can be helpful to be reminded that they're not alone and that others share similar challenges. Many of these poems describe not only such intensely personal struggles but also tell of the ways in which their writers have turned things around to find moments of inner peace and calm. Though they might not characterize it as such, the poets are often describing strategies for shifting the mood, be that immersing themselves in nature, going for a walk or getting some fresh air, reading a book, recalling happy memories, meditating, going to a favourite or safe space, or spending time in solitude or with others.

This is a book of poetry and not a self-help manual, so what is it specifically about poetry that might help the reader? The poets featured in this anthology offer us a huge range of responses from which the reader can find their own meaning. But it is the quality, originality and intensity of the language that is key to creating impact. Rather than an analysis or description of psychological symptoms, poets provide tough and honest words and phrases: 'I am the self-consumer of my woes' (John Clare's 'I am!'), 'Things fall apart; the centre cannot hold' (W B Yeats's 'The Second Coming') and 'It is the hour of disarray/That catches you alone' (Will Eaves's 'Home').

Instead of bullet points of strategies, poets write with powerful and personal directness of the healing power of being in nature. Wendell Berry writes 'I come into the peace of wild things/who do not tax their lives with forethought' and Wordsworth paints a word picture with the memorable phrase 'It is a beauteous evening calm and free'. It is also important to notice not just the world around us but our own sense of being: Thich Nhat Hanh describes the meditative qualities of breathing but in poetic language, 'Breathing in. I have become space/ without boundaries', while for Emily Dickinson breathing the summer air is intoxicating, 'Inebriate of air – am I/And Debauchee of Dew – Reeling – thro' endless summer days'. Elizabeth Barrett Browning talks of the consolation of pets, crediting her dog Flush for her recovery from ill health, 'with my hand upon his head,/Is my benediction said/ Therefore, and for ever'. For Paul Laurence Dunbar it is the ethereal quality of birds descending angelic-like into our human world that offers the promise of relaxation if only we could notice them: 'birds of peace and hope and love/Come fluttering earthward from above,/To settle on life's window-sills,/And ease our load of earthly ills'.

If we would like poetry to be our companion during rocky times, it is important for us to strive to be attentive and receptive readers. We must allow the words to transport us, for us to share the imaginative world created by these poets, to have faith in the experiences they recount and the stories that they have created. If we can do this, if we immerse ourselves in the sounds and rhythms of the verse (even better if we read the poems aloud so that we ourselves are voicing the words, and their cadences can be heard), mind, body and soul can process the poetry more deeply and meaningfully, and our own inner chatter may quieten. Perhaps we will feel a moment of stillness, notice the beginnings of a feeling of calm, or a growing sense of expansion in these little poem-worlds.

Finally, we could let the poetry lead us to taking action: encourage us to take a walk, breathe more slowly and mindfully, seek out companionship, read more widely or deeply, find self-expression by writing our own words or, ultimately, as Joy Harjo exhorts her readers (in the poem 'For Calling the Spirit Back From Wandering the Earth in Its Human Feet'), 'help the next person find the way through the dark'.

The Peace of Wild Things

When despair for the world grows in me
and I wake in the night at the least sound
in fear of what my life and my children's lives
  may be,
I go and lie down where the wood drake
rests in his beauty on the water, and the great
  heron feeds.
I come into the peace of wild things
who do not tax their lives with forethought
of grief. I come into the presence of still water.
And I feel above me the day-blind stars
waiting with their light. For a time
I rest in the grace of the world, and am free.

Wendell Berry (b.1934)

Come, Rest Awhile

Come, rest awhile, and let us idly stray
In glimmering valleys, cool and far away.

Come from the greedy mart, the troubled street,
And listen to the music, faint and sweet,

That echoes ever to a listening ear,
Unheard by those who will not pause to hear –

The wayward chimes of memory's pensive bells,
Windblown o'er misty hills and curtained dells.

One step aside and dewy buds unclose
The sweetness of the violet and the rose;

Song and romance still linger in the green,
Emblossomed ways by you so seldom seen,

And near at hand, would you but see them, lie
All lovely things beloved in days gone by.

You have forgotten what it is to smile
In your too busy life – come, rest awhile.

Lucy Maud Montgomery (1874-1942)

The House Was Quiet and The World Was Calm

The house was quiet and the world was calm.
The reader became the book; and summer night

Was like the conscious being of the book.
The house was quiet and the world was calm.

The words were spoken as if there was no book,
Except that the reader leaned above the page,

Wanted to lean, wanted much most to be
The scholar to whom his book is true, to whom

The summer night is like a perfection of thought.
The house was quiet because it had to be.

The quiet was part of the meaning, part of the mind:
The access of perfection to the page.

And the world was calm. The truth in a calm world,
In which there is no other meaning, itself

Is calm, itself is summer and night, itself
Is the reader leaning late and reading there.

Wallace Stevens (1879-1955)

Music and Sweet Poetry
Fragment

How sweet it is to sit and read the tales
Of mighty poets, and to hear the while
Sweet music, which when the attention fails
Fills the dim pause!

Percy Bysshe Shelley (1792–1822)

Hymn to Time

Time says 'Let there be'
every moment and instantly
there is space and the radiance
of each bright galaxy.

And eyes beholding radiance.
And the gnats' flickering dance.
And the seas' expanse.
And death, and chance.

Time makes room
for going and coming home
and in time's womb
begins all ending.

Time is being and being
time, it is all one thing,
the shining, the seeing,
the dark abounding.

Ursula K Le Guin (1929–2018)

This, Too, Shall Pass Away

When some great sorrow, like a mighty river,
  Flows through your life with peace-destroying
    power,
And dearest things are swept from sight forever,
  Say to your heart each trying hour:
      'This, too, shall pass away.'

When ceaseless toil has hushed your song of
  gladness,
  And you have grown almost too tired to pray,
Let this truth banish from your heart its sadness,
  And ease the burdens of each trying day:
      'This, too, shall pass away.'

When fortune smiles, and, full of mirth and pleasure,
  The days are flitting by without a care,
Lest you should rest with only earthly treasure,
  Let these few words their fullest import bear:
      'This, too, shall pass away.'

When earnest labor brings you fame and glory,
  And all earth's noblest ones upon you smile,
Remember that life's longest, grandest story
  Fills but a moment in earth's little while:
      'This, too, shall pass away.'

Lanta Wilson Smith (1856–1939)

Breathing

Breathing in,
I see myself as a flower.
I am the freshness
of a dewdrop.
Breathing out,
my eyes have become flowers.
Please look at me.
I am looking
with the eyes of love.

Breathing in,
I am a mountain,
imperturbable,
still,
alive,
vigorous.
Breathing out,
I feel solid.
The waves of emotion
can never carry me away.

Breathing in,
I am still water.
I reflect the sky
faithfully.
Look, I have a full moon
within my heart,
the refreshing moon of the bodhisattva.
Breathing out,
I offer the perfect reflection
of my mirror-mind.

Breathing in,
I have become space
without boundaries.
I have no plans left.
I have no luggage.
Breathing out,
I am the moon
that is sailing through the sky of utmost emptiness.
I am freedom.

Thich Nhat Hanh (1926-2022)

‘The quiet mind is richer than a crown’

Sweet are the thoughts that savour of content
Robert Greene

I taste a liquor never brewed

I taste a liquor never brewed –
From Tankards scooped in Pearl –
Not all the Frankfort Berries
Yield such an Alcohol!

Inebriate of air – am I –
And Debauchee of Dew –
Reeling – thro' endless summer days –
From inns of molten Blue –

When 'Landlords' turn the drunken Bee
Out of the Foxglove's door –
When Butterflies – renounce their 'drams' –
I shall but drink the more!

Till Seraphs swing their snowy Hats –
And Saints – to windows run –
To see the little Tippler
Leaning against the – Sun!

Emily Dickinson (1830–1886)

Here's a bottle and an honest friend

Here's a bottle and an honest friend!
  What wad ye wish for mair, man?
Wha kens, before his life may end,
  What his share may be o' care, man.
Then catch the moments as they fly,
  And use them as ye ought, man:
Believe me, happiness is shy,
  And comes not ay when sought, man.

Robert Burns (1759-1796)

Care Took Wing

Adapted from Letter 1, ***A Short Residence in Sweden, Norway and Denmark***

Little patches of earth
Enamelled with the sweetest wild flowers –

Spontaneous pleasure
Gives credibility
To our expectation of happiness.

Lighted up afresh,
Care took wing –
While simple fellow-feeling
Expanded my heart.

Mary Wollstonecraft (1759-1797)

Home

Birds wake to a daily loss of care
And sing the measure of the dawn,
The reddening width of your eyelid,
The world while I was being born.

It is the hour of disarray
That catches you alone in bed,
A prey to all the visitors
Who come and go inside your head

Until a woman's voice downstairs
Topples the crates of memory.
The clattered light behind a blind
Is like responsibility.

Lie quietly. Be unafraid.
We come upon the world undressed
With each rising – it doesn't mind
And this is not another test.

Will Eaves (b.1967)

Out in the Fields With God

The little cares that fretted me
I lost them yesterday
Among the fields, above the sea,
Among the winds at play,
Among the lowing of the herds,
The rustling of the trees,
Among the singing of the birds,
The humming of the bees.

The foolish fears of what might happen,
I cast them all away
Among the clover-scented grass,
Among the new-mown hay,
Among the husking of the corn,
Where drowsy poppies nod,
Where ill thoughts can die and good be born –
Out in the fields with God.

Attributed to Elizabeth Barrett Browning (1806–1861)

Advice

W'en you full o' worry
  'Bout yo' wo'k an' sich,
W'en you kind o' bothered
  Case you can't get rich,
An' yo' neighboh p'ospah
  Past his jest desu'ts,
An' de sneer of comerds
  Stuhes yo' heaht an' hu'ts,
Des don' pet yo' worries,
  Lay 'em on de she'f,
Tek a little trouble
  Brothah, wid yo'se'f.

Ef a frien' comes mou'nin'
  'Bout his awful case,
You know you don' grieve him
  Wid a gloomy face,
But you wrassle wid him,
  Try to tek him in;
Dough hit cracks yo' features,
  Law, you smile lak sin,
Ain't you good ez he is?
  Don' you pine to def;
Tek a little trouble
  Brothah, wid yo'se'f.

Ef de chillun pestahs,
  An' de baby's bad,
Ef yo' wife gits narvous,
  An' you're gettin' mad,
Des you grab yo' boot-strops,
  Hol' yo' body down,
Stop a-tinkin' cuss-w'rds,
  Chase away de frown,
Knock de haid o' worry,
  Twell dey ain' none lef';
Tek a little trouble,
  Brothah, wid yo'se'f.

Paul Laurence Dunbar (1872-1906)

Comrades

I and my Soul are alone to-day,
All in the shining weather;
We were sick of the world, and put it away,
So we could rejoice together.

Our host, the Sun, in the blue, blue sky
Is mixing a rare, sweet wine,
In the burnished gold of this cup on high,
For me, and this Soul of mine.

We find it a safe and a royal drink,
And a cure for every pain:
It helps us to love, and helps us to think,
And strengthens body and brain.

And sitting here, with my Soul alone,
Where the yellow sun-rays fall,
Of all the friends I have ever known
I find it the *best* of all.

We rarely meet when the World is near,
  For the World hath a pleasing art,
And brings me so much that is bright and dear
  That my Soul it keepeth apart.

But when I grow weary of mirth and glee,
  Of glitter, glow, and splendour,
Like a tried old friend it comes to me,
  With a smile that is sad and tender.

And we walk together as two friends may,
  And laugh and drink God's wine.
Oh, a royal comrade any day
  I find this Soul of mine.

Ella Wheeler Wilcox (1850–1919)

The World is Too Much With Us

The world is too much with us; late and soon,
Getting and spending, we lay waste our powers; –
Little we see in Nature that is ours;
We have given our hearts away, a sordid boon!
This Sea that bares her bosom to the moon;
The winds that will be howling at all hours,
And are up-gathered now like sleeping flowers;
For this, for everything, we are out of tune;
It moves us not. Great God! I'd rather be
A Pagan suckled in a creed outworn;
So might I, standing on this pleasant lea,
Have glimpses that would make me less forlorn;
Have sight of Proteus rising from the sea;
Or hear old Triton blow his wreathèd horn.

William Wordsworth (1770–1850)

Ode to a Nightingale

Verses 1–2 and 4–5

My heart aches, and a drowsy numbness pains
  My sense, as though of hemlock I had drunk,
Or emptied some dull opiate to the drains
  One minute past, and Lethe-wards had sunk:
'Tis not through envy of thy happy lot,
  But being too happy in thine happiness, –
    That thou, light-wingèd Dryad of the trees
      In some melodious plot
  Of beechen green, and shadows numberless,
    Singest of summer in full-throated ease.

O, for a draught of vintage! that hath been
  Cool'd a long age in the deep-delved earth,
Tasting of Flora and the country green,
  Dance, and Provençal song, and sunburnt mirth!
O for a beaker full of the warm South,
  Full of the true, the blushful Hippocrene,
    With beaded bubbles winking at the brim,
      And purple-stained mouth;
  That I might drink, and leave the world unseen,
    And with thee fade away into the forest dim:

Away! away! for I will fly to thee,
Not charioted by Bacchus and his pards,
But on the viewless wings of Poesy,
Though the dull brain perplexes and retards:
Already with thee! tender is the night,
And haply the Queen-Moon is on her throne,
Cluster'd around by all her starry Fays;
But here there is no light,
Save what from heaven is with the breezes blown
Through verdurous glooms and winding
mossy ways.

I cannot see what flowers are at my feet,
Nor what soft incense hangs upon the boughs,
But, in embalmed darkness, guess each sweet
Wherewith the seasonable month endows
The grass, the thicket, and the fruit-tree wild;
White hawthorn, and the pastoral eglantine;
Fast fading violets cover'd up in leaves;
And mid-May's eldest child,
The coming musk-rose, full of dewy wine,
The murmurous haunt of flies on
summer eves.

John Keats (1795–1821)

'the broad sun Is sinking down in its tranquillity'

It is a beauteous Evening, calm and free
William Wordsworth

Laughing Song

When the green woods laugh with the voice of joy,
And the dimpling stream runs laughing by;
When the air does laugh with our merry wit,
And the green hill laughs with the noise of it;

When the meadows laugh with lively green,
And the grasshopper laughs in the merry scene,
When Mary and Susan and Emily
With their sweet round mouths sing 'Ha, Ha He!'

When the painted birds laugh in the shade,
Where our table with cherries and nuts is spread,
Come live, and be merry, and join with me,
To sing the sweet chorus of 'Ha, Ha, He!'

William Blake (1757–1827)

Sonnet 29

When, in disgrace with fortune and men's eyes,
I all alone beweep my outcast state,
And trouble deaf heaven with my bootless cries,
And look upon myself and curse my fate,
Wishing me like to one more rich in hope,
Featured like him, like him with friends possessed,
Desiring this man's art and that man's scope,
With what I most enjoy contented least;
Yet in these thoughts myself almost despising,
Haply I think on thee, and then my state,
(Like to the lark at break of day arising
From sullen earth) sings hymns at heaven's gate;
  For thy sweet love remembered such wealth brings
  That then I scorn to change my state with kings.

William Shakespeare (1564–1616)

The Miller of the Dee

There dwelt a miller, hale and bold,
  Beside the river Dee;
He worked and sang from morn till night,
  No lark more blithe than he.
And this the burden of his song
  Forever used to be, –
'I envy nobody, no, not I,
  And nobody envies me!'

'Thou'rt wrong, my friend,' said old King Hal,
  'Thou'rt wrong, as wrong can be;
For could my heart be light as thine,
  I'd gladly change with thee.
And tell me now, what makes thee sing
  With voice so loud and free,
While I am sad, though I am king,
  Beside the river Dee?'

The miller smiled and doffed his cap,
  'I earn my bread,' quoth he;
'I love my wife, I love my friend,
  I love my children three;
I owe no penny I cannot pay;
  I thank the river Dee,
That turns the mill and grinds the corn
  That feeds my babes and me.'

‘Good friend,’ said Hal, and sighed the while,
‘Farewell, and happy be;
But say no more, if thou’dst be true,
That no one envies thee:
Thy mealy cap is worth my crown,
Thy mill my kingdom’s fee;
Such men as thou are England’s boast,
O miller of the Dee!’

Charles Mackay (1814–1889)

‘the ancient forest trees Talked together in the breeze’

The Trees’ Counselling
Christina Rossetti

Fairy Bread

Come up here, O dusty feet!
  Here is fairy bread to eat.
Here in my retiring room,
  Children, you may dine
On the golden smell of broom
  And the shade of pine;
And when you have eaten well,
Fairy stories hear and tell.

Robert Louis Stevenson (1850–1894)

Wine of the Fairies

Fragment

I am drunk with the honey wine
Of the moon-unfolded eglantine,
Which fairies catch in hyacinth bowls.
The bats, the dormice, and the moles
Sleep in the walls or under the sward
Of the desolate castle yard;
And when 'tis spilt on the summer earth
Or its fumes arise among the dew,
Their jocund dreams are full of mirth,
They gibber their joy in sleep; for few
Of the fairies bear those bowls so new!

Percy Bysshe Shelley (1792–1822)

The Absinthe Drinker

Gently I wave the visible world away.
  Far off, I hear a roar, afar yet near,
  Far off and strange, a voice is in my ear,
And is the voice my own? the words I say
Fall strangely, like a dream, across the day;
  And the dim sunshine is a dream. How clear,
  New as the world to lovers' eyes, appear
The men and women passing on their way!

The world is very fair. The hours are all
  Linked in a dance of mere forgetfulness.
      I am at peace with God and man. O glide,
Sands of the hour-glass that I count not, fall
  Serenely: scarce I feel your soft caress.
      Rocked on this dreamy and indifferent tide.

Arthur Symons (1865–1945)

Winter Night

Pile high the hickory and the light
Log of chestnut struck by the blight.
Welcome-in the winter night.

The day has gone in hewing and felling,
Sawing and drawing wood to the dwelling
For the night of talk and story-telling.

These are the hours that give the edge
To the blunted axe and the bent wedge,
Straighten the saw and lighten the sledge.

Here are question and reply,
And the fire reflected in the thinking eye.
So peace, and let the bob-cat cry.

Edna St Vincent Millay (1892–1950)

‘Like a cat asleep on a chair at peace’

Pax
D H Lawrence

When de Co'n Pone's Hot

Dey is times in life when Nature
Seems to slip a cog an' go,
Jes' a-rattlin' down creation,
Lak an ocean's overflow;
When de worl' jes' stahts a-spinnin'
Lak a picaninny's top,
An' yo' cup o' joy is brimmin'
'Twell it seems about to slop,
An' you feel jes' lak a racah,
Dat is trainin' fu' to trot –
When yo' mammy says de blessin'
An' de co'n pone's hot.

When you set down at de table,
Kin' o' weary lak an' sad,
An' you'se jes' a little tiahed
An' purhaps a little mad;
How yo' gloom tu'ns into gladness,
How yo' joy drives out de doubt
When de oven do' is opened,
An' de smell comes po'in' out;
Why, de 'lectric light o' Heaven
Seems to settle on de spot,
When yo' mammy says de blessin'
An' de co'n pone's hot.

When de cabbage pot is steamin'
An' de bacon good an' fat,
When de chittlins is a-sputter'n'
So's to show you whah dey's at;
Tek away yo' sody biscuit,
Tek away yo' cake an' pie,
Fu' de glory time is comin',
An' it's 'proachin' mighty nigh,
An' you want to jump an' hollah,
Dough you know you'd bettah not,
When yo' mammy says de blessin'
An' de co'n pone's hot.

I have hyeahd a' lots o' sermons,
An' I've hyeahd o' lots o' prayers,
An I've listened to some singin'
Dat has tuck me up de stairs
Of de Glory-Lan' an' set me
Jes' below de Mastah's th'one,
An' have lef' my hea't a-singin'
In a happy aftah tone;
But dem wu'ds so sweetly murmured
Seem to tech de softes' spot,
When my mammy says de blessin',
An' de co'n pone's hot.

Paul Laurence Dunbar (1872–1906)

Let Evening Come

Let the light of late afternoon
shine through chinks in the barn, moving
up the bales as the sun moves down.

Let the cricket take up chafing
as a woman takes up her needles
and her yarn. Let evening come.

Let dew collect on the hoe abandoned
in long grass. Let the stars appear
and the moon disclose her silver horn.

Let the fox go back to its sandy den.
Let the wind die down. Let the shed
go black inside. Let evening come.

To the bottle in the ditch, to the scoop
in the oats, to air in the lung
let evening come.

Let it come, as it will, and don't
be afraid. God does not leave us
comfortless, so let evening come.

Jane Kenyon (1947–1995)

The Gift of Life

Life is a night all dark and wild,
Yet still stars shine:
This moment is a star, my child –
Your star and mine.

Life is a desert dry and drear,
Undewed, unblest;
This hour is an oasis, dear;
Here let us rest.

Life is a sea of windy spray,
Cold, fierce and free:
An isle enchanted is to-day
For you and me.

Forget night, sea, and desert: take
The gift supreme,
And, of life's brief relenting, make
A deathless dream.

E Nesbit (1858–1924)

Pied Beauty

Glory be to God for dappled things –
For skies of couple-colour as a brinded cow;
For rose-moles all in stipple upon trout
that swim;
Fresh-firecoal chestnut-falls; finches' wings;
Landscape plotted and pieced – fold, fallow, and
plough;
And áll trádes, their gear and tackle and trim.

All things counter, original, spare, strange;
Whatever is fickle, freckled (who knows how?)
With swift, slow; sweet, sour; adazzle, dim;
He fathers-forth whose beauty is past change:
Praise him.

Gerard Manley Hopkins (1844–1889)

The Throne of Osiris

In the roof the swallow has built her nest,
  And the martins under the eaves,
And all wingèd things have a chamber of rest
  In the shadow of swaying leaves.

The rabbit has dug for himself a hole,
  The green worm lies at the heart of the rose,
And there is rest for the vagrant soul
  Wherever the shallowest river flows.

Eva Gore-Booth (1870–1926)

To Flush, My Dog

Extract

But of thee it shall be said,
This dog watched beside a bed
Day and night unweary, –
Watched within a curtained room,
Where no sunbeam brake the gloom
Round the sick and dreary.

Roses, gathered for a vase,
In that chamber died apace,
Beam and breeze resigning –
This dog only, waited on,
Knowing that when light is gone,
Love remains for shining.

Other dogs in thymy dew
Tracked the hares and followed through
Sunny moor or meadow –
This dog only, crept and crept
Next a languid cheek that slept,
Sharing in the shadow.

Therefore to this dog will I,
Tenderly not scornfully,
Render praise and favour!

With my hand upon his head,
Is my benediction said
Therefore, and for ever.

And because he loves me so,
Better than his kind will do
Often, man or woman,
Give I back more love again
Than dogs often take of men, –
Leaning from my Human.

Blessings on thee, dog of mine,
Pretty collars make thee fine,
Sugared milk make fat thee!
Pleasures wag on in thy tail –
Hands of gentle motion fail
Nevermore, to pat thee!

Downy pillow take thy head,
Silken coverlid bestead,
Sunshine help thy sleeping!
No fly's buzzing wake thee up –
No man break thy purple cup,
Set for drinking deep in.

Mock I thee, in wishing weal? –
Tears are in my eyes to feel
Thou art made so straightly,
Blessing needs must straighten too, –
Little canst thou joy or do,
Thou who lovest greatly.

Yet be blessed to the height
Of all good and all delight
Pervious to thy nature, –
Only loved beyond that line,
With a love that answers thine,
Loving fellow-creature!

Elizabeth Barrett Browning (1806–1861)

On the Grasshopper and Cricket

The poetry of earth is never dead:
When all the birds are faint with the hot sun,
And hide in cooling trees, a voice will run
From hedge to hedge about the new-mown mead:
That is the grasshopper's – he takes the lead
In summer luxury, – he has never done
With his delights, for when tired out with fun,
He rests at ease beneath some pleasant weed
The poetry of earth is ceasing never:
On a lone winter evening, when the frost
Has wrought a silence, from the stove there shrills
The Cricket's song, in warmth increasing ever,
And seems to one in drowsiness half lost,
The Grasshopper's among some grassy hills.

John Keats (1795–1821)

Leisure

What is this life if, full of care,
We have no time to stand and stare.

No time to stand beneath the boughs
And stare as long as sheep or cows.

No time to see, when woods we pass,
Where squirrels hide their nuts in grass.

No time to see, in broad daylight,
Streams full of stars, like skies at night.

No time to turn at Beauty's glance,
And watch her feet, how they can dance.

No time to wait till her mouth can
Enrich that smile her eyes began.

A poor life this is if, full of care,
We have no time to stand and stare.

W H Davies (1871-1940)

Pax

All that matters is to be at one with the living God
to be a creature in the house of the God of Life.

Like a cat asleep on a chair
at peace, in peace
and at one with the master of the house, with
the mistress,
at home, at home in the house of the living,
sleeping on the hearth, and yawning before the fire.

Sleeping on the hearth of the living world
yawning at home before the fire of life
feeling the presence of the living God
like a great reassurance
a deep calm in the heart
a presence
as of the master sitting at the board
in his own and greater being,
in the house of life.

D H Lawrence (1885-1930)

Labours Leisure

O for the feelings and the carless health
That found me toiling in the fields – the joy
I felt at eve with not a wish for wealth
When labour done and in the hedge put bye
My delving spade – I homeward used to hie
With thoughts of books I often read by stealth
Beneath the blackthorn clumps at dinners hour
It urged my weary feet with eager speed
To hasten home where winter fires did shower
Scant light now felt as beautiful indeed
Where bending oer my knees I used to read
With earnest heed all books that had the power
To give me joy in most delicious ways
And rest my spirits after weary days

Aye when long summer showers lets labour win
Sweet leisure – how I used to mark with joy
The south grow black and blacker to the eye
Till the rain came and pessed me to the skin
No matter anxious happiness was bye
With her refreshing pictures through the rain
Carless of bowering bush and sheltering tree
I homeward hied to feed on books again

For they were then a very feast to me
The simplest things were sweetest melody
And nothing met my eager taste in vain
And thus to read I often wished for rain
Such leisure fancys fed my lowly lot
Possessing nothing and still wanting not

It is an happiness that simplest hearts
Find their own joy in what they undertake
That nature like the seasons so imparts
That every mind its own home comfort makes
That be our dwelling in the fields or woods
No matter custom so endears the scenes
We feel in lonliness sweet company
And many a varied pleasure intervenes
Which the wide world unnoting passes bye
Pursuing what delights it varied joy
Thus happiness is with us joys succeed
Spontaneous everywhere like summer weeds
The cheerful commoners of every spot
Blessing the highest and the lowliest lot

John Clare (1793–1864)

Enquiry After Peace
Fragment

Peace! where art thou to be found?
Where, in all the spacious Round,
May thy Footsteps be pursu'd?
Where may thy calm Seats be view'd?
On some Mountain dost thou lie,
Serenely near the ambient Sky,
Smiling at the Clouds below,
Where rough Storms and Tempests grow?
Or, in some retired Plain,
Undisturb'd dost thou remain?
Where no angry Whirlwinds pass,
Where no Floods oppress the Grass.
High above, or deep below,
Fain I thy Retreat wou'd know.
Fain I thee *alone* wou'd find,
Balm to my o'er-weary'd Mind.
Since what here the World enjoys,
Or our Passions most employs,
Peace opposes, or destroys.
Pleasure's a tumultuous thing,
Busy still, and still on Wing;
Flying swift, from place to place,

Darting from each beauteous Face;
From each strongly mingled Bowl
Through th'inflam'd and restless Soul.
Sov'reign Pow'r who fondly craves,
But himself to Pomp enslaves;
Stands the Envy of Mankind,
Peace, in vain, attempts to find.
Thirst of Wealth no Quiet knows,
But near the Death-bed fiercer grows;
Wounding Men with secret Stings,
For Evils it on Others brings.
War who not discreetly shuns,
Thorough Life the Gauntlet runs.
Swords, and Pikes, and Waves, and Flames,
Each their Stroke against him aims.
Love (if such a thing there be)
Is all Despair, or Extasie.
Poetry's the feav'rish Fit,
Th' o'erflowing of unbounded Wit. &c.

Anne Finch, Countess of Winchilsea (1661–1720)

Thoughts on My Sick-Bed
Verses 1–3 and 8–13

And has the remnant of my life
Been pilfered of this sunny Spring?
And have its own prelusive sounds
Touched in my heart no echoing string?

Ah! say not so – the hidden life
Couchant within this feeble frame
Hath been enriched by kindred gifts,
That, undesired, unsought-for, came

With joyful heart in youthful days
When fresh each season in its Round
I welcomed the earliest Celandine
Glittering upon the mossy ground;

Yet never in those careless days
When spring-time in rock, field, or bower
Was but a fountain of earthly hope
A promise of fruits & the splendid flower.

No! then I never felt a bliss
That might with that compare
Which, piercing to my couch of rest,
Came on the vernal air.

When loving Friends an offering brought,
The first flowers of the year,
Culled from the precincts of our home,
From nooks to Memory dear.

With some sad thoughts the work was done.
Unprompted and unbidden,
But joy it brought to my hidden life,
To consciousness no longer hidden.

I felt a Power unfelt before,
Controlling weakness, languor, pain;
It bore me to the Terrace walk
I trod the Hills again; –

No prisoner in this lonely room,
I saw the green Banks of the Wye,
Recalling thy prophetic words,
Bard, Brother, Friend from infancy!

No need of motion, or of strength,
Or even the breathing air;
– I thought of Nature's loveliest scenes;
And with Memory I was there.

Dorothy Wordsworth (1771–1855)

‘tranquil depths reflect a tranquil sky’

Winged Words
Mary Elizabeth Coleridge

Freedom

Give me the long, straight road before me,
  A clear, cold day with a nipping air,
Tall, bare trees to run on beside me,
  A heart that is light and free from care.
Then let me go! – I care not whither
  My feet may lead, for my spirit shall be
Free as the brook that flows to the river,
  Free as the river that flows to the sea.

Olive Runner (dates unknown)

The Retreat

Happy those early days! when I
Shined in my angel infancy.
Before I understood this place
Appointed for my second race,
Or taught my soul to fancy aught
But a white, celestial thought;
When yet I had not walked above
A mile or two from my first love,
And looking back, at that short space,
Could see a glimpse of His bright face;
When on some gilded cloud or flower
My gazing soul would dwell an hour,
And in those weaker glories spy
Some shadows of eternity;
Before I taught my tongue to wound
My conscience with a sinful sound,
Or had the black art to dispense
A several sin to every sense,
But felt through all this fleshly dress
Bright shoots of everlastingness.

O, how I long to travel back,
And tread again that ancient track!
That I might once more reach that plain
Where first I left my glorious train,
From whence th' enlightened spirit sees
That shady city of palm trees.
But, ah! my soul with too much stay
Is drunk, and staggers in the way.
Some men a forward motion love;
But I by backward steps would move,
And when this dust falls to the urn,
In that state I came, return.

Henry Vaughan (1621-1695)

A Dream
Extract

Was it a dream? We sail'd, I thought we sail'd,
Martin and I, down a green Alpine stream,
Under o'erhanging pines; the morning sun,
On the wet umbrage of their glossy tops,
On the red pinings of their forest floor,
Drew a warm scent abroad; behind the pines
The mountain skirts, with all their sylvan change
Of bright-leaf'd chestnuts, and moss'd walnut-trees,
And the frail scarlet-berried ash, began.
Swiss chalets glitter'd on the dewy slopes,
And from some swarded shelf high up, there came
Notes of wild pastoral music: over all
Rang'd, diamond-bright, the eternal wall of snow.
Upon the mossy rocks at the stream's edge,
Back'd by the pines, a plank-built cottage stood,
Bright in the sun; the climbing gourd-plant's leaves
Muffled its walls, and on the stone-strewn roof
Lay the warm golden gourds; golden, within,
Under the eaves, peer'd rows of Indian corn.

Matthew Arnold (1822–1888)

Digging (2)

Today I think
Only with scents, – scents dead leaves yield,
And bracken, and wild carrot's seed,
And the square mustard field;

Odours that rise
When the spade wounds the root of tree,
Rose, currant, raspberry, or goutweed,
Rhubarb or celery;

The smoke's smell, too,
Flowing from where a bonfire burns
The dead, the waste, the dangerous,
And all to sweetness turns.

It is enough
To smell, to crumble the dark earth,
While the robin sings over again
Sad songs of Autumn mirth.

Edward Thomas (1878–1917)

All Day It Has Rained

All day it has rained, and we on the edge of the
  moors
Have sprawled in our bell-tents, moody and dull as
  boors,
Groundsheets and blankets spread on the muddy
  ground
And from the first grey wakening we have found
No refuge from the skirmishing fine rain
And the wind that made the canvas heave and flap
And the taut wet guy-ropes ravel out and snap.
All day the rain has glided, wave and mist and
  dream,
Drenching the gorse and heather, a gossamer stream
Too light to stir the acorns that suddenly
Snatched from their cups by the wild south-westerly
Pattered against the tent and our upturned dreaming
  faces.
And we stretched out, unbuttoning our braces,
Smoking a Woodbine, darning dirty socks,
Reading the Sunday papers – I saw a fox
And mentioned it in the note I scribbled home; –
And we talked of girls, and dropping bombs on
  Rome,

And thought of the quiet dead and the loud
celebrities
Exhorting us to slaughter, and the herded refugees;
– Yet thought softly, morosely of them, and as
indifferently
As of ourselves or those whom we
For years have loved, and will again
Tomorrow maybe love; but now it is the rain
Possesses us entirely, the twilight and the rain.
And I can remember nothing dearer or more to
my heart
Than the children I watched in the woods on
Saturday
Shaking down burning chestnuts for the schoolyard's
merry play,
Or the shaggy patient dog who followed me
By Sheet and Steep and up the wooded scree
To the Shoulder o' Mutton where Edward Thomas
brooded long
On death and beauty – till a bullet stopped his song.

Alun Lewis (1915–1944)

Retirement
Hymn

Far from the World, O Lord I flee,
  From strife, and tumult far,
From scenes, where Satan wages still
  His most successful war.

The calm retreat, the silent shade,
  With prayer, and praise agree;
And seem, by thy sweet bounty made,
  For those, who follow Thee.

There, if thy Spirit touch the Soul,
  And grace her mean abode,
O with what peace, and joy, and love,
  She communes with her God!

There, like the nightingale she pours
  Her solitary lays;
Nor asks a witness of her song,
  Nor thirsts, for human praise.

Author, and Guardian of my life,
  Sweet source of light divine,
And (all harmonious names, in one)
  My Saviour Thou art mine!

What thanks I owe Thee, and what love,
  A boundless, endless store;
Shall echo through the realms above,
  When time shall be no more.

William Cowper (1731-1800)

Grongar Hill

Lines 131-158

Content me with an humble shade,
My passions tam'd, my wishes laid;
For while our wishes wildly roll,
We banish quiet from the soul;
'Tis thus the busy beat the air,
And misers gather wealth and care.
  Now, ev'n now, my joys run high,
As on the mountain-turf I lie;
While the wanton Zephyr sings,
And in the vale perfumes his wings;
While the waters murmur deep;
While the shepherd charms his sheep;
While the birds unbounded fly,
And with music fill the sky,
Now, ev'n now, my joys run high.

Be full, ye Courts! be great who will;
Search for peace with all your skill:
Open wide the lofty door,
Seek her on the marble floor:
In vain ye search, she is not there;
In vain ye search the domes of Care!
Grass and flowers Quiet treads,
On the meads and mountain-heads,
Along with pleasure close ally'd,
Ever by each other's side,
And often, by the murm'ring rill,
Hears the thrush, while all is still,
Within the groves of Grongar Hill.

John Dyer (1699–1757)

Lines Written in Early Spring

I heard a thousand blended notes,
While in a grove I sate reclined,
In that sweet mood when pleasant thoughts
Bring sad thoughts to the mind.

To her fair works did Nature link
The human soul that through me ran;
And much it grieved my heart to think
What man has made of man.

Through primrose tufts, in that green bower,
The periwinkle trailed its wreaths;
And 'tis my faith that every flower
Enjoys the air it breathes.

The birds around me hopped and played,
Their thoughts I cannot measure: –
But the least motion which they made,
It seemed a thrill of pleasure.

The budding twigs spread out their fan,
To catch the breezy air;
And I must think, do all I can,
That there was pleasure there.

If this belief from heaven be sent,
If such be Nature's holy plan,
Have I not reason to lament
What man has made of man?

William Wordsworth (1770-1850)

‘The
foolish
fears of
what might
happen, I
cast them
all away’

Out in the Fields With God
Elizabeth Barrett Browning

Now Sleeps the Crimson Petal

From *The Princess*

Now sleeps the crimson petal, now the white;
Nor waves the cypress in the palace walk;
Nor winks the gold fin in the porphyry font.
The firefly wakens; waken thou with me.

  Now droops the milk-white peacock like a ghost,
And like a ghost she glimmers on to me.

  Now lies the Earth all Danaë to the stars,
And all thy heart lies open unto me.

  Now slides the silent meteor on, and leaves
A shining furrow, as thy thoughts in me.

  Now folds the lily all her sweetness up,
And slips into the bosom of the lake.
So fold thyself, my dearest, thou, and slip
Into my bosom and be lost in me.

Alfred, Lord Tennyson (1809-1892)

A Boat Beneath a Sunny Sky

A boat, beneath a sunny sky,
Lingering onward dreamily
In an evening of July –

Children three that nestle near,
Eager eye and willing ear,
Pleased a simple tale to hear –

Long has paled that sunny sky:
Echoes fade and memories die:
Autumn frosts have slain July.

Still she haunts me, phantomwise,
Alice moving under skies
Never seen by waking eyes.

Children yet, the tale to hear,
Eager eye and willing ear,
Lovingly shall nestle near.

In a Wonderland they lie,
Dreaming as the days go by,
Dreaming as the summers die:

Ever drifting down the stream –
Lingering in the golden gleam –
Life, what is it but a dream?

Lewis Carroll (1832–1898)

By lone St. Mary's silent lake

By lone St. Mary's silent lake:
Thou know'st it well, – nor fen nor sedge
Pollute the pure lake's crystal edge;
Abrupt and sheer, the mountains sink
At once upon the level brink;
And just a trace of silver sand
Marks where the water meets the land.
Far in the mirror, bright and blue,
Each hill's huge outline you may view;
Shaggy with heath, but lonely bare,
Nor tree, nor bush, nor brake, is there,
Save where, of land, yon slender line
Bears thwart the lake the scatter'd pine.
Yet even this nakedness has power,
And aids the feeling of the hour:
Nor thicket, dell, nor copse you spy,
Where living thing concealed might lie;
Nor point, retiring, hides a dell,
Where swain, or woodman lone, might dwell;
There's nothing left to fancy's guess,
You see that all is loneliness:
And silence aids – though the steep hills
Send to the lake a thousand rills;
In summer tide, so soft they weep,
The sound but lulls the ear asleep;
Your horse's hoof-tread sounds too rude,
So stilly is the solitude.

Sir Walter Scott (1771–1832)

Donnybrook

I saw the moon, so broad and bright,
Sailing high on a frosty night!

And the air shone silvery between
The pearly queen, and the silver queen!

And here a white, and there a white
Cloud-mist swam in a mist of light!

And, all encrusted in the sky,
High, and higher, and yet more high,

Were golden star-points glimmering through
The hollow vault, the vault of blue!

And then I knew – that God was good,
And the world was fair! And, where I stood,

I bent the knee, and bent the head;
And said my prayers, and went to bed.

James Stephens (1880–1950)

The Shining Light

My former hopes are fled,
  My terror now begins;
I feel, alas! that I am dead
  In trespasses and sins.

Ah, whither shall I fly?
  I hear the thunder roar;
The law proclaims destruction nigh,
  And vengeance at the door.

When I review my ways,
  I dread impending doom:
But sure a friendly whisper says,
  'Flee from the wrath to come!'

I see, or think I see,
  A glimmering from afar!
A beam of day, that shines for me,
  To save me from despair.

Forerunner of the sun,
  It marks the pilgrim's way;
I'll gaze upon it while I run,
  And watch the rising day.

William Cowper (1731-1800)

O Solitude! if I must with thee dwell
Sonnet VII

O Solitude! if I must with thee dwell,
Let it not be among the jumbled heap
Of murky buildings; climb with me the steep, –
Nature's observatory – whence the dell,
Its flowery slopes, its river's crystal swell,
May seem a span; let me thy vigils keep
'Mongst boughs pavillion'd, where the deer's
  swift leap
Startles the wild bee from the fox-glove bell.
But though I'll gladly trace these scenes with thee,
Yet the sweet converse of an innocent mind,
Whose words are images of thoughts refin'd,
Is my soul's pleasure; and it sure must be
Almost the highest bliss of human-kind,
When to thy haunts two kindred spirits flee.

John Keats (1795–1821)

The Child in the Garden

When to the garden of untroubled thought
  I came of late, and saw the open door,
  And wished again to enter, and explore
The sweet, wild ways with stainless bloom inwrought,
And bowers of innocence with beauty fraught,
  It seemed some purer voice must speak before
  I dared to tread that garden loved of yore,
That Eden lost unknown and found unsought.

Then just within the gate I saw a child, –
  A stranger-child, yet to my heart most dear;
He held his hands to me, and softly smiled
  With eyes that knew no shade of sin or fear:
'Come in,' he said, 'and play awhile with me;'
'I am the little child you used to be.'

Henry Van Dyke (1852–1933)

The Wood

Verses 1-3

But two miles more, and then we rest!
Well, there is still an hour of day,
And long the brightness of the West
Will light us on our devious way;
Sit then, awhile, here in this wood –
So total is the solitude,
  We safely may delay.

These massive roots afford a seat,
Which seems for weary travellers made.
There rest. The air is soft and sweet
In this sequestered forest glade,
And there are scents of flowers around,
The evening dew draws from the ground;
  How soothingly they spread!

Yes; I was tired, but not at heart;
No – that beats full of sweet content,
For now I have my natural part
Of action with adventure blent;
Cast forth on the wide world with thee,
And all my once waste energy
  To weighty purpose bent.

Charlotte Brontë (1816-1855)

Forest

In fact, the trees are murmuring under your feet,
a buried empathy; you tread it.
                                        High over your head,
the canopy sieves light; a conversation
you lip-read. The forest
                                        keeps different time;
slow hours as long as your life,
so you feel human.
So you feel more human; persuaded what you are
by wordless breath of wood, reason in resin.
You might name them –
                                        oak, ash, holly, beech, elm –
but the giants are silence alive, superior,
and now you are all instinct;
swinging the small lamp of your heart
as you venture their world:
the green, shadowy, garlic air
                                        your ancestors breathed.
Ah, you thought love human
till you lost yourself in the forest,
but it is more strange.
                                        These grave and patient saints
who pray and pray
and suffer your little embrace.

Carol Ann Duffy (b.1955)

Adlestrop

Yes. I remember Adlestrop –
The name, because one afternoon
Of heat the express-train drew up there
Unwontedly. It was late June.

The steam hissed. Someone cleared his throat.
No one left and no one came
On the bare platform. What I saw
Was Adlestrop – only the name

And willows, willow-herb, and grass,
And meadowsweet, and haycocks dry,
No whit less still and lonely fair
Than the high cloudlets in the sky.

And for that minute a blackbird sang
Close by, and round him, mistier,
Farther and farther, all the birds
Of Oxfordshire and Gloucestershire.

Edward Thomas (1878-1917)

‘sing the sweet chorus of ‘Ha, Ha, He!’ ’

Laughing Song
William Blake

Get a Transfer

If you are on the Gloomy Line,
Get a transfer.
If you're inclined to fret and pine,
Get a transfer.
Get off the track of doubt and gloom,
Get on the Sunshine Track – there's room –
Get a transfer.

If you're on the Worry Train,
Get a transfer.
You must not stay there and complain,
Get a transfer.
The Cheerful Cars are passing through,
And there's lots of room for you –
Get a transfer.

If you're on the Grouchy Track,
Get a transfer.
Just take a Happy Special back,
Get a transfer.
Jump on the train and pull the rope,
That lands you at the station of Hope –
Get a transfer.

Anon

The Peninsula

When you have nothing more to say, just drive
For a day all around the peninsula.
The sky is tall as over a runway,
The land without marks, so you will not arrive

But pass through, though always skirting landfall.
At dusk, horizons drink down sea and hill,
The ploughed field swallows the whitewashed gable
And you're in the dark again. Now recall

The glazed foreshore and silhouetted log.
That rock where breakers shredded into rags,
The leggy birds stilted on their own legs,
Islands riding themselves out into the fog.

And drive back home, still with nothing to say
Except that now you will uncode all landscapes
By this: things founded clean on their own shapes,
Water and ground in their extremity.

Seamus Heaney (1939–2013)

All seasons shall be sweet to thee

From *Frost at Midnight*

            …all seasons shall be sweet to thee,
Whether the summer clothe the general earth
With greenness, or the redbreast sit and sing
Betwixt the tufts of snow on the bare branch
Of mossy apple-tree, while the nigh thatch
Smokes in the sun-thaw; whether the eave-drops fall
Heard only in the trances of the blast,
Or if the secret ministry of frost
Shall hang them up in silent icicles,
Quietly shining to the quiet Moon.

Samuel Taylor Coleridge (1772–1834)

On a Lane in Spring

A little lane – the brook runs close beside,
  And spangles in the sunshine while the fish glide
    swiftly by
And hedges leafing with the green springtide;
  From out their greenery the old birds fly,
And chirp and whistle in the morning sun;
  The pilewort glitters 'neath the pale blue sky,
The little robin has its nest begun,
  And grass-green linnets round the bushes fly.
How mild the spring comes in! the daisy buds
  Lift up their golden blossoms to the sky.
How lovely are the pingles and the woods!
  Here a beetle runs – and there a fly
Rests on the arum leaf in bottle-green
  And all the spring in this Sweet lane is seen.

John Clare (1793-1864)

Summer Night Piece

The garden is steeped in moonlight,
Full to its high edges with brimming silver,
And the fish-ponds brim and darken
And run in little serpent lights soon extinguished.
Lily-pads lie upon the surface, beautiful as the
  tarnishings on frail old silver,
And the Harvest moon droops heavily out of the sky,
A ripe, white melon, intensely, magnificently, shining.
Your window is orange in the moonlight,
It glows like a lamp behind the branches of the old
  wistaria,
It burns like a lamp before a shrine,
The small, intimate, familiar shrine
Placed reverently among the bricks
Of a much-loved garden wall.

Amy Lowell (1874-1925)

Long Island Sound

I see it as it looked one afternoon
In August, – by a fresh soft breeze o'erblown.
The swiftness of the tide, the light thereon,
A far-off sail, white as a crescent moon.
The shining waters with pale currents strewn,
The quiet fishing-smacks, the Eastern cove,
The semi-circle of its dark, green grove.
The luminous grasses, and the merry sun
In the grave sky; the sparkle far and wide,
Laughter of unseen children, cheerful chirp
Of crickets, and low lisp of rippling tide,
Light summer clouds fantastical as sleep
Changing unnoted while I gazed thereon.
All these fair sounds and sights I made my own.

Emma Lazarus (1849-1887)

‘Search for Peace with all your skill’

Grongar Hill
John Dyer

The Broken Gate

I know a little broken gate
  Beneath the apple-boughs and pines,
The seasons lend it coloured state,
  And round its hinge the ivy twines –
The ivy and the bloomless rose,
  And autumn berries flaming red;
The pine its gracious scent bestows,
  The apple-boughs their treasure shed.

It opens on an orchard hung
  With heavy-laden boughs that spill
Their brown and yellow fruit among
  The withered stems of daffodil:
The river from its shallows freed
  Here falls upon a stirless peace,
The tides of time suspended lead
  The tired spirit to release.

A little land of mellowed ease
  I find beyond my broken gate,
I hear amid the laden trees
  A magic song, and there elate
I pass along from sound and sight
  Of men who fret the world away, –
I gather rich and rare delight
  Where every day is holy day.

John Drinkwater (1882–1937)

Autumn River Song

On the Broad Reach

In the clear green water – the shimmering moon.
In the moonlight – white herons flying.
A young man hears a girl plucking water-chestnuts;
They paddle home together through the night,
  singing.

Li Bai (701–762)
Translated by Florence Ayscough (1878–1942)
and Amy Lowell (1874–1925)

Reply to an Unrefined Person Encountered in the Hills

He asks why I perch in the green jade hills.
I smile and do not answer. My heart is comfortable
and at peace.
Fallen peach-flowers spread out widely, widely, over
the water.
It is another sky and earth, not the world of man.

Li Bai (701–762)
Translated by Florence Ayscough (1878–1942)
and Amy Lowell (1874–1925)

The door

Go and open the door.
Maybe outside there's
a tree, or a wood,
a garden,
or a magic city.

Go and open the door.
Maybe a dog's rummaging.
Maybe you'll see a face,
or an eye,
or the picture
of a picture.

Go and open the door.
If there's a fog
it will clear.

Go and open the door.
Even if there's only
the darkness ticking,
even if there's only
the hollow wind,
even if
nothing
is there,
go and open the door.

At least
there'll be
a draught.

Miroslav Holub (1923–1998)
Translated from the Czech by Ian Milner (1911–1991)

On Reason and Passion

From *The Prophet*

And the priestess spoke again and said: Speak to us
of Reason and Passion.
And he answered, saying:
Your soul is oftentimes a battlefield, upon which
your reason and your judgement wage war
against your passion and your appetite.
Would that I could be the peacemaker in your soul,
that I might turn the discord and the rivalry of
your elements into oneness and melody.
But how shall I, unless you yourselves be also the
peacemakers, nay, the lovers of all your elements?
…
Among the hills, when you sit in the cool shade of
the white poplars, sharing the peace and serenity
of distant fields, and meadows – then let your
heart say in silence, 'God rests in reason.'
And when the storm comes, and the mighty wind
shakes the forest, and thunder and lightning
proclaim the majesty of the sky, – then let your
heart say in awe, 'God moves in passion.'
And since you are a breath in God's sphere, and a
leaf in God's forest, you too should rest in reason
and move in passion.

Kahlil Gibran (1883–1931)

The Second Coming

Turning and turning in the widening gyre
The falcon cannot hear the falconer;
Things fall apart; the centre cannot hold;
Mere anarchy is loosed upon the world,
The blood-dimmed tide is loosed, and everywhere
The ceremony of innocence is drowned;
The best lack all conviction, while the worst
Are full of passionate intensity.

Surely some revelation is at hand;
Surely the Second Coming is at hand.
The Second Coming! Hardly are those words out
When a vast image out of *Spiritus Mundi*
Troubles my sight: somewhere in sands of the desert
A shape with lion body and the head of a man,
A gaze blank and pitiless as the sun,
Is moving its slow thighs, while all about it
Reel shadows of the indignant desert birds.
The darkness drops again; but now I know
That twenty centuries of stony sleep
Were vexed to nightmare by a rocking cradle,
And what rough beast, its hour come round at last,
Slouches towards Bethlehem to be born?

W B Yeats (1865-1939)

The Sparrow

A little bird, with plumage brown,
Beside my window flutters down,
A moment chirps its little strain,
Ten taps upon my window-pane,
And chirps again, and hops along,
To call my notice to its song;
But I work on, nor heed its lay,
Till, in neglect, it flies away.

So birds of peace and hope and love
Come fluttering earthward from above,
To settle on life's window-sills,
And ease our load of earthly ills;
But we, in traffic's rush and din
Too deep engaged to let them in,
With deadened heart and sense plod on,
Nor know our loss till they are gone.

Paul Laurence Dunbar (1872–1906)

The Gift to Sing

Sometimes the mist overhangs my path,
And blackening clouds about me cling;
But, oh, I have a magic way
To turn the gloom to cheerful day –
  I softly sing.

And if the way grows darker still,
Shadowed by Sorrow's somber wing,
With glad defiance in my throat,
I pierce the darkness with a note,
  And sing, and sing.

I brood not over the broken past,
Nor dread whatever time may bring;
No nights are dark, no days are long,
While in my heart there swells a song,
  And I can sing.

James Weldon Johnson (1871-1938)

A Violin at Dusk

Stumble to silence, all you uneasy things,
That pack the day with bluster and with fret.
For here is music at each window set;
Here is a cup which drips with all the springs
That ever bud a cowslip flower; a roof
To shelter till the argent weathers break;
A candle with enough of light to make
My courage bright against each dark reproof.
A hand's width of clear gold, unraveled out
The rosy sky, the little moon appears;
As they were splashed upon the paling red,
Vast, blurred, the village poplars lift about.
I think of young, lost things: of lilacs; tears;
I think of an old neighbor, long since dead.

Lizette Woodworth Reese (1856–1935)

To Memory

Strange Power, I know not what thou art,
Murderer or mistress of my heart.
I know I'd rather meet the blow
Of my most unrelenting foe
Than live – as now I live – to be
Slain twenty times a day by thee.

Yet, when I would command thee hence,
Thou mockest at the vain pretence,
Murmuring in mine ear a song
Once loved, alas! forgotten long;
And on my brow I feel a kiss
That I would rather die than miss.

Mary Elizabeth Coleridge (1861-1907)

I Wandered Lonely as a Cloud

I wandered lonely as a cloud
That floats on high o'er vales and hills,
When all at once I saw a crowd,
A host, of golden daffodils;
Beside the lake, beneath the trees,
Fluttering and dancing in the breeze.

Continuous as the stars that shine
And twinkle on the milky way,
They stretched in never-ending line
Along the margin of a bay:
Ten thousand saw I at a glance,
Tossing their heads in sprightly dance.

The waves beside them danced; but they
Out-did the sparkling waves in glee:
A poet could not but be gay,
In such a jocund company:
I gazed – and gazed – but little thought
What wealth the show to me had brought:

For oft, when on my couch I lie
In vacant or in pensive mood,
They flash upon that inward eye
Which is the bliss of solitude;
And then my heart with pleasure fills,
And dances with the daffodils.

William Wordsworth (1770-1850)

I Am!

I am! yet what I am none cares or knows,
My friends forsake me like a memory lost;
I am the self-consumer of my woes,
They rise and vanish in oblivious host,
Like shades in love and death's oblivion lost;
And yet I am! and live with shadows tost

Into the nothingness of scorn and noise,
Into the living sea of waking dreams,
Where there is neither sense of life nor joys,
But the vast shipwreck of my life's esteems;
And e'en the dearest – that I loved the best –
Are strange – nay, rather stranger than the rest.

I long for scenes where man has never trod;
A place where woman never smil'd or wept;
There to abide with my creator, God,
And sleep as I in childhood sweetly slept:
Untroubling and untroubled where I lie;
The grass below – above the vaulted sky.

John Clare (1793–1864)

The Hours

Those hours are best when suddenly
The voices of the world are still,
And in that quiet place is heard
The voice of one small singing bird,
Alone within his quiet tree;

When to one field that crowns a hill,
With but the sky for neighbourhood,
The crowding counties of my brain
Give all their riches, lake and plain,
Cornland and fell and pillared wood;
When in a hill-top acre, bare
For the seed's use, I am aware
Of all the beauty that an age
Of earth has taught my eyes to see;

When Pride and Generosity
The Constant Heart and Evil Rage,
Affection and Desire, and all

The passions of experience
Are no more tabled in my mind,
Learning's idolatry, but find
Particularity of sense
In daily fortitudes that fall
From this or that companion,
Or in an angry gossip's word;

When one man speaks for Every One,
When Music lives in one small bird,
When in a furrowed hill we see
All beauty in epitome –
Those hours are best; for those belong
To the lucidity of song.

John Drinkwater (1882–1937)

‘Sit then, awhile, here in this wood’

The Wood
Charlotte Brontë

The stars are mansions built by Nature's hand

The stars are mansions built by Nature's hand,
And, haply, there the spirits of the blest
Dwell, clothed in radiance, their immortal vest;
Huge Ocean shows, within his yellow strand,
A habitation marvellously planned,
For life to occupy in love and rest;
All that we see – is dome, or vault, or nest,
Or fortress, reared at Nature's sage command.
Glad thought for every season! but the Spring
Gave it while cares were weighing on my heart,
'Mid song of birds, and insects murmuring;
And while the youthful year's prolific art –
Of bud, leaf, blade, and flower – was fashioning
Abodes where self-disturbance hath no part.

William Wordsworth (1770–1850)

The Old Vicarage, Grantchester

Extract

Café des Westens, Berlin, May 1912

Ah God! to see the branches stir
Across the moon at Grantchester!
To smell the thrilling-sweet and rotten
Unforgettable, unforgotten
River-smell, and hear the breeze
Sobbing in the little trees.
Say, do the elm-clumps greatly stand
Still guardians of that holy land?
The chestnuts shade, in reverend dream,
The yet unacademic stream?
Is dawn a secret shy and cold
Anadyomene, silver-gold?
And sunset still a golden sea

From Haslingfield to Madingley?
And after, ere the night is born,
Do hares come out about the corn?
Oh, is the water sweet and cool,
Gentle and brown, above the pool?
And laughs the immortal river still
Under the mill, under the mill?
Say, is there Beauty yet to find?
And Certainty? and Quiet kind?
Deep meadows yet, for to forget
The lies, and truths, and pain? … oh! yet
Stands the Church clock at ten to three?
And is there honey still for tea?

Rupert Brooke (1887–1915)

For Calling the Spirit Back from Wandering the Earth in Its Human Feet

Put down that bag of potato chips, that white bread,
 that bottle of pop.

Turn off that cellphone, computer, and remote control.

Open the door, then close it behind you.

Take a breath offered by friendly winds. They travel
the earth gathering essences of plants to clean.

Give it back with gratitude.

If you sing it will give your spirit lift to fly to the stars'
 ears and back.

Acknowledge this earth who has cared for you since
 you were a dream planting itself precisely within your
 parents' desire.

Let your moccasin feet take you to the encampment of
 the guardians who have known you before time, who
 will be there after time. They sit before the fire that
 has been there without time.

Let the earth stabilize your postcolonial insecure jitters.

Be respectful of the small insects, birds and animal people who accompany you.
Ask their forgiveness for the harm we humans have brought down upon them.

Don't worry.
The heart knows the way though there may be high-rises, interstates, checkpoints, armed soldiers, massacres, wars, and those who will despise you because they despise themselves.

The journey might take you a few hours, a day, a year, a few years, a hundred, a thousand or even more.

Watch your mind. Without training it might run away and leave your heart for the immense human feast set by the thieves of time.

Do not hold regrets.

When you find your way to the circle, to the fire kept burning by the keepers of your soul, you will be welcomed.

You must clean yourself with cedar, sage, or other healing plant.

Cut the ties you have to failure and shame.

Let go the pain you are holding in your mind, your shoulders, your heart, all the way to your feet. Let go the pain of your ancestors to make way for those who are heading in our direction.

Ask for forgiveness.

Call upon the help of those who love you. These helpers take many forms: animal, element, bird, angel, saint, stone, or ancestor.

Call your spirit back. It may be caught in corners and creases of shame, judgment, and human abuse.

You must call in a way that your spirit will want to return.
Speak to it as you would to a beloved child.

Welcome your spirit back from its wandering. It may return in pieces, in tatters. Gather them together. They will be happy to be found after being lost for so long.

Your spirit will need to sleep awhile after it is bathed and given clean clothes.

Now you can have a party. Invite everyone you know
who loves and supports you. Keep room for those
who have no place else to go.

Make a giveaway, and remember, keep the speeches
short.

Then, you must do this: help the next person find their
way through the dark.

Joy Harjo (b.1951)

Praying

It doesn't have to be
the blue iris, it could be
weeds in a vacant lot, or a few
small stones; just
pay attention, then patch

a few words together and don't try
to make them elaborate, this isn't
a contest but the doorway

into thanks, and a silence in which
another voice may speak.

Mary Oliver (1935–2019)

Thought

Thought, I love thought.
But not the jiggling and twisting of already existent ideas
I despise that self-important game.
Thought is the welling up of unknown life into consciousness,
Thought is the testing of statements on the touchstone of consciousness,
Thought is gazing onto the face of life, and reading what can be read,
Thought is pondering over experience, and coming to conclusion.
Thought is not a trick, or an exercise, or a set of dodges,
Thought is a man in his wholeness, wholly attending.

D H Lawrence (1885–1930)

O for a Booke

O for a Booke and a shadie nooke,
  eyther in-a-doore or out;
With the grene leaves whispering overhede,
  or the Streete cryes all about.
Where I maie Reade all at my ease,
  both of the Newe and Olde;
For a jollie goode Booke whereon to looke
Is better to me than Golde.

Anon

‘Quietly shining to the quiet Moon’

Frost at Midnight
Samuel Taylor Coleridge

I stood tiptoe upon a little hill

Extract

I stood tiptoe upon a little hill,
The air was cooling, and so very still,
That the sweet buds which with a modest pride
Pull droopingly, in slanting curve aside,
Their scantly leaved, and finely tapering stems,
Had not yet lost their starry diadems
Caught from the early sobbing of the morn.
The clouds were pure and white as flocks new-shorn,
And fresh from the clear brook; sweetly they slept
On the blue fields of heaven, and then there crept
A little noiseless noise among the leaves,
Born of the very sigh that silence heaves;
For not the faintest motion could be seen
Of all the shades that slanted o'er the green.
There was wide wandering for the greediest eye,

To peer about upon variety;
Far round the horizon's crystal air to skim,
And trace the dwindled edgings of its brim;
To picture out the quaint, and curious bending
Of a fresh woodland alley never ending:
Or by the bowery clefts, and leafy shelves,
Guess where the jaunty streams refresh themselves.
I gazed awhile, and felt as light, and free
As though the fanning wings of Mercury
Had play'd upon my heels: I was light-hearted,
And many pleasures to my vision started;
So I straightway began to pluck a posey
Of luxuries bright, milky, soft and rosy.

John Keats (1795–1821)

The Thrush's Nest

Within a thick and spreading hawthorn bush,
  That overhung a molehill large and round,
I heard from morn to morn a merry thrush
  Sing hymns to sunrise, and I drank the sound
With joy; and often, an intruding guest,
  I watched her secret toil from day to day –
How true she warped the moss to form a nest,
  And modelled it within with wood and clay;
And by and by, like heath-bells gilt with dew,
  There lay her shining eggs, as bright as flowers,
Ink-spotted over shells of greeny blue;
  And there I witnessed, in the sunny hours
A brood of nature's minstrels chirp and fly,
  Glad as the sunshine and the laughing sky.

John Clare (1793–1864)

Afternoon on a Hill

I will be the gladdest thing
  Under the sun!
I will touch a hundred flowers
  And not pick one.

I will look at cliffs and clouds
  With quiet eyes,
Watch the wind bow down the grass,
  And the grass rise.

And when lights begin to show
  Up from the town,
I will mark which must be mine,
  And then start down!

Edna St Vincent Millay (1892–1950)

The Word

Down near the bottom
of the crossed-out list
of things you have to do today,

between 'green thread'
and 'broccoli,' you find
that you have penciled 'sunlight.'

Resting on the page, the word
is beautiful. It touches you
as if you had a friend

and sunlight were a present
he had sent from someplace distant
as this morning – to cheer you up,

and to remind you that,
among your duties, pleasure
is a thing

that also needs accomplishing.
Do you remember?
that time and light are kinds

of love, and love
is no less practical
than a coffee grinder

or a safe spare tire?
Tomorrow you may be utterly
without a clue,

but today you get a telegram
from the heart in exile,
proclaiming that the kingdom

still exists,
the king and queen alive,
still speaking to their children,

– to any one among them
who can find the time
to sit out in the sun and listen.

Tony Hoagland (1953–2018)

A Shady Spot

Adapted from *Recollections of Ilfracombe*

We looked at the sunlight
living like a spirit
among the branches
of the hanging woods.

Looked too at a caterpillar
which happened to be spending
its transitional life,
happily knowing
nothing of transitions,
on the bush beside us.

George Eliot (1819-1880)

Interludes

Not a beginning, not an end,
this neutral place
is rich with stillness,
with movement in all directions.
In the word of the prophet, we
are travellers. So pass in peace, stranger,
though our orbits differ,
I too have rested here at these
limbo interludes
in our shared planet's rotation.
So catch your breath and let my words
welcome you like a friend's blessing.
May this space around you expand
and glow in the warmth of knowing
that it's only a corridor;
not a beginning, not an end,
but a green oasis.

Debjani Chatterjee (b.1952)

The Trees' Counselling

I was strolling sorrowfully
  Thro' the corn fields and the meadows;
The stream sounded melancholy,
  And I walked among the shadows;
While the ancient forest trees
Talked together in the breeze;
In the breeze that waved and blew them,
With a strange weird rustle thro' them.

Said the oak unto the others
  In a leafy voice and pleasant:
'Here we all are equal brothers,
  'Here we have nor lord nor peasant.
'Summer, Autumn, Winter, Spring,
'Pass in happy following.
'Little winds may whistle by us,
'Little birds may overfly us;

'But the sun still waits in heaven
  'To look down on us in splendour;
'When he goes the moon is given,
  'Full of rays that he doth lend her:
'And tho' sometimes in the night
'Mists may hide her from our sight,
'She comes out in the calm weather,
'With the glorious stars together.'

From the fruitage, from the blossom,
  From the trees came no denying;
Then my heart said in my bosom:
  'Wherefore art thou sad and sighing?
'Learn contentment from this wood
'That proclaimeth all states good;
'Go not from it as it found thee;
'Turn thyself and gaze around thee.'

And I turned: behold the shading
  But showed forth the light more clearly;
The wild bees were honey-lading;
  The stream sounded hushing merely,
And the wind not murmuring
Seemed, but gently whispering:
'Get thee patience; and thy spirit
'Shall discern in all things merit.'

Christina Rossetti (1830–1894)

Psalm 130

De Profundis clamavi

Extract

From depth of sin and from a deep despair,
  From depth of death, from depth of heart's sorrow,
  From this deep cave of darkness deep repair,
Thee have I called, O Lord, to be my borrow;
  Thou in my voice, O Lord, perceive and hear
  My heart, my hope, my plaint, my overthrow,
My will to rise: and let by grant appear
  That to my voice Thine ears do well intend.
  No place so far that to Thee is not near;
No depth so deep that Thou ne mayst extend
  Thine ear thereto: hear then my woeful plaint.
  For, Lord, if Thou do observe what men offend
And put Thy native mercy in restraint,
  If just exaction demand recompense,
  Who may endure, O Lord? Who shall not faint

At such accompt? Dread, and not reverence
  Should so reign large. But Thou seeks rather love.
  For in Thy hand is mercy's residence,
By hope whereof Thou dost our hearts move.
  I in Thee, Lord, have set my confidence;
  My soul such trust doth evermore approve.
Thy holy word of eterne excellence,
  Thy mercy's promise that is alway just,
  Have been my stay, my pillar and pretense.
My soul in God hath more desirous trust
  Than hath the watchman looking for the day,
  By the relief to quench of sleep the thrust.

Sir Thomas Wyatt (1503–1542)

The Guest House

This being human is a guest house.
Every morning a new arrival.

A joy, a depression, a meanness,
some momentary awareness comes
as an unexpected visitor.

Welcome and entertain them all!
Even if they're a crowd of sorrows,
who violently sweep your house
empty of its furniture,
still, treat each guest honorably.
He may be clearing you out
for some new delight.

The dark thought, the shame, the malice,
meet them at the door laughing,
and invite them in.

Be grateful for whoever comes,
because each has been sent
as a guide from beyond.

Rumi (1207–1273)
Translated from the Persian by Coleman Barks (b. 1937)

Sweet are the thoughts that savour of content

Sweet are the thoughts that savour of content;
The quiet mind is richer than a crown;
Sweet are the nights in careless slumber spent;
The poor estate scorns fortune's angry frown:
Such sweet content, such minds, such sleep,
  such bliss,
Beggars enjoy, when princes oft do miss.
The homely house that harbours quiet rest;
The cottage that affords no pride nor care;
The mean that 'grees with country music best;
The sweet consort of mirth and music's fare;
Obscurèd life sets down a type of bliss:
A mind content both crown and kingdom is.

Robert Greene (c.1558–1592)

A Ballad to Mrs Catherine Fleming in London from Malshanger Farm in Hampshire

Extract

From me, who whiloem sung the Town,
  This second Ballad comes;
To let you know we are got down,
  From hurry, smoke, and drums:
And every visitor that rowls,
In restless Coach from Mall to Paul's,
  With a fa-la-la-la-la-la.

And now were I to paint the seat,
  (As well-bred poets use;)
I shou'd embellish our retreat,
  By favour of the muse:
Tho' to no villa we pretend,
But a plain farm at the best end.
  With a fa-la &c.

For jarring sounds in London streets,
  Which still are passing by;
Where cowcumbers with Sand ho meets,
  And for loud mastery vie:
The driver whistling to his team,
Here wakes us from some rural dream.
  With a fa-la &c.

We silver trouts and Cray-fish eat,
  Just taken from the stream;
And never think our meal compleat,
  Without fresh curds and cream:
And as we pass by the barn floor,
We choose our supper from the door.
With a fa-la &c.

Mean while accept what I have writ,
  To shew this rural scene;
Nor look for sharp satyrick wit,
  From off the balmy plain:
The country breeds no thorny bays,
But mirth and love and honest praise.
  With a fa-la-la-la-la-la.

Anne Finch, Countess of Winchilsea (1661–1720)

The Crystal Gazer

I shall gather myself into myself again,
  I shall take my scattered selves and make them one,
Fusing them into a polished crystal ball
  Where I can see the moon and the flashing sun.

I shall sit like a sibyl, hour after hour intent,
  Watching the future come and the present go,
And the little shifting pictures of people rushing
  In restless self-importance to and fro.

Sara Teasdale (1884-1933)

The Lake Isle of Innisfree

I will arise and go now, and go to Innisfree,
And a small cabin build there, of clay and wattles
  made:
Nine bean-rows will I have there, a hive for the
  honey-bee;
And live alone in the bee-loud glade.

And I shall have some peace there, for peace comes
  dropping slow,
Dropping from the veils of the morning to where the
  cricket sings;
There midnight's all a glimmer, and noon a purple
  glow,
And evening full of the linnet's wings.

I will arise and go now, for always night and day
I hear lake water lapping with low sounds by the
  shore;
While I stand on the roadway, or on the pavements
  grey,
I hear it in the deep heart's core.

W B Yeats (1865–1939)

Long years have left their writing on my brow

Long years have left their writing on my brow,
But yet the freshness and the dew-fed beam
Of those young mornings are about me now,
When we two wandered toward the far-off stream

With rod and line. Our basket held a store
Baked for us only, and I thought with joy
That I should have my share, though he had more,
Because he was the elder and a boy.

The firmaments of daisies since to me
Have had those mornings in their opening eyes,
The bunchèd cowslip's pale transparency
Carries that sunshine of sweet memories,

And wild-rose branches take their finest scent
From those blest hours of infantine content.

George Eliot (1819-1880)

It is a beauteous Evening, calm and free

It is a beauteous Evening, calm and free,
The holy time is quiet as a Nun
Breathless with adoration; the broad sun
Is sinking down in its tranquillity;
The gentleness of heaven broods o'er the Sea;
Listen! the mighty Being is awake,
And doth with his eternal motion make
A sound like thunder – everlastingly.
Dear Child! dear Girl! that walkest with me here,
If thou appear untouched by solemn thought,
Thy nature is not therefore less divine:
Thou liest in Abraham's bosom all the year;
And worshipp'st at the Temple's inner shrine,
God being with thee when we know it not.

William Wordsworth (1770–1850)

Winged Words

As darting swallows skim across a pool,
  Whose tranquil depths reflect a tranquil sky,
So, o'er the depths of silence, dark and cool,
        Our winged words dart playfully,
          And seldom break
        The quiet surface of the lake,
          As they flit by.

Mary Elizabeth Coleridge (1861-1907)

The Laughing Heart

your life is your life
don't let it be clubbed into dank submission.
be on the watch.
there are ways out.
there is a light somewhere.
it may not be much light but
it beats the darkness.
be on the watch.
the gods will offer you chances.
know them.
take them.
you can't beat death but
you can beat death in life, sometimes.
and the more often you learn to do it,
the more light there will be.
your life is your life.
know it while you have it.
you are marvelous
the gods wait to delight
in you.

Charles Bukowski (1920–1994)

The fresh air

From 'Week-End' sonnet sequence

VII.

The fresh air moves like water round a boat.
  The white clouds wander. Let us wander too.
The whining, wavering plover flap and float.
  That crow is flying after that cuckoo.
Look! Look! … they're gone. What are the great trees
 calling?
  Just come a little farther, by that edge
Of green, to where the stormy ploughland, falling
  Wave upon wave, is lapping to the hedge.
Oh, what a lovely bank! Give me your hand.
  Lie down and press your heart against the ground.
Let us both listen till we understand
  Each through the other, every natural sound …

      I can't hear anything today, can you,
      But, far and near: 'Cuckoo! Cuckoo!
  Cuckoo!'?

Harold Monro (1879–1932)

Love after Love

The time will come
when, with elation,
you will greet yourself arriving
at your own door, in your own mirror
and each will smile at the other's welcome,

and say, sit here. Eat.
You will love again the stranger who was your self.
Give wine. Give bread, Give back your heart
to itself, to the stranger who has loved you

all your life, whom you ignored
for another, who knows you by heart.
Take down the love letters from the bookshelf

the photographs, the desperate notes,
peel your own image from the mirror.
Sit. Feast on your life.

Derek Walcott (1930–2017)

The Fall of Foyers

Loch Ness, Inverness-Shire

I.

Wet with the spray of this transcendant river,
  Upon this crag with mosses cover'd o'er,
I love to stand, and listen to the roar
Of waters bursting down the rocks for ever –
Dash'd into rainbows where the sunbeams quiver.
  The sound of billows as they beat the shore,
  Or thunder leaping on the hill-tops hoar,
Till the firm earth beneath its footsteps shiver,
Is not more awful than thy flood, O Foyers!
  Roaring 'mid chasms like an escaping sea –
  Alone, and silent, in thy presence vast,
Awed, yet elated, the rapt soul aspires,
  Forgetting all its meaner longings past,
To hold high converse, intimate, with thee.

II.

Yes! all unmindful of the world without,
  My spirit with thee, and my eyes in thrall
To thy great beauty, swathing me about.
  To me thy voice breathes peace, majestic Fall!
  Envy and pride, and warring passions all –
Hatred and scorn, and littleness of mind,
And all the mean vexations of mankind,
  Fade from my spirit at thy powerful call.
I stand before thee, reverent and dumb.
  And hear thy voice discoursing to my soul
  Sublime orations tuned to psalmody –
High thoughts of peril met and overcome –
  Of Power and Beauty and Eternity,
And the great God who bade thy waters roll!

Charles Mackay (1814–1889)

Thus I went wide-where, walking alone

From 'The Vision of Do-Well' in *Piers Plowman*

Thus I went wide-where, walking alone,
In a wide wilderness, by a wood side.
Bliss of the birds song made me abide there,
And on a lawn under a linden I leaned awhile
To listen to their lays, their lovely notes;
The mirth of their mouths made me to sleep.
And mid that bliss I dreamed – marvellously.

William Langland (c. 1330–c. 1400)
Translated from Middle English by Arthur Burrell (1859–1946)

'How sweet it is to sit and read'

Music and Sweet Poetry
Percy Bysshe Shelley

Walking
Verses 4–9

To walk is by a thought to go;
To move in spirit to and fro;
To mind the good we see;
To taste the sweet;
Observing all the things we meet
How choice and rich they be.

To note the beauty of the day,
And golden fields of corn survey;
Admire each pretty flow'r
With its sweet smell;
To praise their Maker, and to tell
The marks of his great pow'r.

To fly abroad like active bees,
Among the hedges and the trees,
To cull the dew that lies
On ev'ry blade,
From ev'ry blossom; till we lade
Our minds, as they their thighs.

Observe those rich and glorious things,
The rivers, meadows, woods, and springs,
The fructifying sun;
To note from far
The rising of each twinkling star
For us his race to run.

A little child these well perceives,
Who, tumbling in green grass and leaves,
May rich as kings be thought,
But there's a sight
Which perfect manhood may delight,
To which we shall be brought.

While in those pleasant paths we talk,
'Tis that tow'rds which at last we walk;
For we may by degrees
Wisely proceed
Pleasures of love and praise to heed,
From viewing herbs and trees.

Thomas Traherne (c.1637-1674)

‘rest my spirits after weary days’

Labours Leisure
John Clare

Index of Poets

Index of First Lines

Sources

Wendell Berry, 'The Peace of Wild Things' from *New Collected Poems*. Copyright © 2012 by Wendell Berry. Reprinted with the permission of The Permissions Company, LLC on behalf of Counterpoint Press, counterpointpress.com. From *The Peace of Wild Things: And Other Poems* (2018) by Wendell Berry, published by Penguin Books Ltd.

'The Laughing Heart', from *The Laughing Heart* by Charles Bukowski (1996), Black Sparrow Press, HarperCollins Publishers. Copyright Linda Lee Bukowski.

'Interludes', from *Namaskar: New & Selected Poems* by Debjani Chatterjee (Redbeck Press, 2004). Reproduced by kind permission of Debjani Chatterjee.

'I taste a liquor never brewed', from THE POEMS OF EMILY DICKINSON: READING EDITION, edited by Ralph W. Franklin, Cambridge, Mass.: The Belknap Press of Harvard University Press, Copyright © 1998, 1999 by the President and Fellows of Harvard College. Copyright © 1951, 1955 by the President and Fellows of Harvard College. Copyright © renewed 1979, 1983 by the President and Fellows of Harvard College. Copyright © 1914, 1918, 1919, 1924, 1929, 1930, 1932, 1935, 1937, 1942 by Martha Dickinson Bianchi. Copyright © 1952, 1957, 1958, 1963, 1965 by Mary L. Hampson. Used by permission. All rights reserved.

'Forest' (2019) by Carol Ann Duffy. Commissioned by Forestry England for their centenary year. Copyright with Carol Ann Duffy through the RCW Literary Agency.

'Home', from *Sound Houses* (2011) by Will Eaves, published by and reproduced by permission of Carcanet Press.

'For Calling the Spirit Back from Wandering the Earth in Its Human Feet', from CONFLICT RESOLUTION FOR HOLY BEINGS: POEMS by Joy Harjo. Copyright © 2015 by Joy Harjo. Used by permission of W. W. Norton & Company, Inc.

'The Peninsula', from *Door into the Dark* (2002) by Seamus Heaney. Published by and reprinted by permission of Faber and Faber Ltd; Farrar, Straus and Giroux, an imprint of Macmillan Publishers.

'The Word' from *Sweet Ruin* by Tony Hoagland (1992), published and reprinted by the University of Wisconsin Press.

'The door', Miroslav Holub, trans. Ian Milner. *Poems Before & After: Collected English Translations*, trans. Ian & Jarmila Milner et al. (Bloodaxe Books, 2006). Reproduced with permission of Bloodaxe Books. www.bloodaxebooks.com @bloodaxebooks (twitter/facebook) #bloodaxebooks

'Let Evening Come', Jane Kenyon, from *Collected Poems*. Copyright © 2005 by The Estate of Jane Kenyon. Reprinted with the permission of The Permissions Company, LLC on behalf of Graywolf Press, graywolfpress.org.

'Hymn to Time', copyright © 2016 by Ursula K Le Guin. First appeared in LATE IN THE DAY, published by PM Press in 2016. Reprinted by permission of Ginger Clark Literary, LLC.

'Breathing', Thich Nhat Hanh, excerpt from *Call Me by My True Names*. Copyright © 2022 by Plum Village Community of Engaged Buddhism, Inc. with the permission of Parallax Press, Berkeley, California, www.parallax.org.

'Praying' from *Thirst: Poems* (2006) by Mary Oliver, reprinted by the permission of The Charlotte Sheedy Literary Agency as agent for the author. Copyright © 2009, 2017 by Mary Oliver with permission of Bill Reichblum.

'The Guest House' from *Rumi: Selected Poems* (2004), Penguin Classics, an imprint of Penguin Books, trans. Coleman Barks, with John Moynce, A. J. Arberry, Reynold Nicholson.

'The House Was Quiet and the World Was Calm' from THE COLLECTED POEMS OF WALLACE STEVENS by Wallace Stevens, copyright © 1954 by Wallace Stevens and copyright renewed 1982 by Holly Stevens. Used by permission of Alfred A. Knopf, an imprint of the Knopf Doubleday Publishing Group, a division of Penguin Random House LLC. All rights reserved. Published by and reprinted by permission of Faber and Faber Ltd.

'Love after Love' from *The Poetry of Derek Walcott 1948-2013* (2014) by Derek Walcott, sel. Glyn Maxwell. Published by and reprinted by permission of Faber and Faber Ltd; Farrar, Straus and Giroux, an imprint of Macmillan Publishers.

Acknowledgements

A very big thank you to the great team at Batsford, particularly to my editors, Magda Simões-Brown and Nicola Newman. Thank you, as ever, to The Reader charity for not only reigniting my own love of literature but also showing me, through the practise of shared reading and reading aloud, how to help people overcome the barriers that sometimes stand in the way of us enjoying and experiencing poetry. Thank you to my family and friends who continue to support and encourage my literary adventures.

About the Editor

Liz Ison studied English Literature at the University of Cambridge. Since 2015, Liz has been leading shared reading groups in person and online as well as workshops encouraging people to enjoy and rediscover poetry. Her poetry anthologies include *100 Poems to Help You Heal* and *A Poem to Read Aloud Every Day of the Year.* Liz lives in London.

First published in the United Kingdom
in 2025 by
Batsford
43 Great Ormond Street
London
WC1N 3HZ

An imprint of B. T. Batsford Holdings Limited

ISBN 978 1 83733 002 7

A CIP catalogue record for this book is available from the British Library.

10 9 8 7 6 5 4 3 2 1

Printed by Toppan Leefung Printing International Ltd, China
Reproduction by Rival Colour Ltd, UK

This book can be ordered direct from the publisher at www.batsfordbooks.com, or try your local bookshop

Distributed throughout the UK and Europe by Abrams & Chronicle Books, 1 West Smithfield, London EC1A 9JU and 57 rue Gaston Tessier, 75166 Paris, France

www.abramsandchronicle.co.uk
info@abramsandchronicle.co.uk